Deer Whisperer

25 years of Raising Whitetails

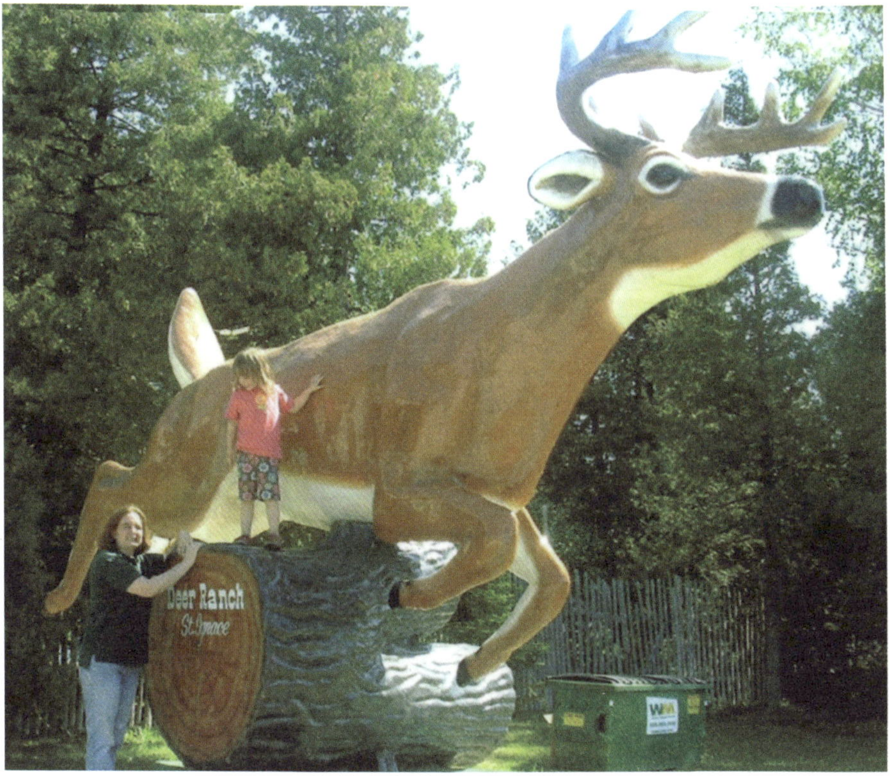

Daughter Dorothy and her niece Kaila

By Harold Kriesche

Harold Kriesche

Deer Whisperer

25 years of Raising Whitetails

By Harold Kriesche

Published by Martin Lake Deer Farm

ISBN # 978-0-615-78534-9

Copyright April 2013 Harold Kriesche

Photography by Harold & Sally Kriesche unless otherwise noted

Cover Photo by Jeff Andrews

Print Coordination, Cover Design and Interior Layout by
Globe Printing, Inc., Ishpeming, MI   www.globeprinting.net

No portion of this publication may be reproduced, reprinted, or otherwise copied for distribution purposes without express written permission of the author and publisher.

Additional books available at

Martin lake Deer Farm
W 1522 E Martin lake Road, St. Ignace, MI 49781
906-643-9311

email: hkriesche@lighthouse.net

Paperback & e-books available
www.DeerWhispererBook.com

Table of Contents

Chapter 1 ~ Getting Started 5
Chapter 2 ~ Changes Are Coming 9
Chapter 3 ~ More Problems 15
Chapter 4 ~ Nature's Ways 19
Chapter 5 ~ Mother Nature Gets Our Fawns 21
Chapter 6 ~ PEPI 25
Chapter 7 ~ Big Boy Shines 31
Chapter 8 ~ Learning the Hard Way 35
Chapter 9 ~ World's Oldest Whitetail............ 39
Chapter 10 ~ Long Toenails & Skinny Does 43
Chapter 11 ~ Tail Biting 47
Chapter 12 ~ Harden Your Heart 49
Chapter 13 ~ TB Testing...................... 53
Chapter 14 ~ Deer Whisperer Gets His Name 57
Chapter 15 ~ Hurricane Winds 61
Chapter 16 ~ White Whitetails 65
Chapter 17 ~ Our Albino Deer 69
Chapter 18 ~ Sierra, Our First Albino Doe......... 77
Chapter 19 ~ Bottle Feeding Fawns 81
Chapter 20 ~ Odds & Ends.................... 87
About the Author Harold Kriesche.............. 95

Dedication

I dedicate this book to my wife Sally. We have been together over 50 years. She built the Deer Ranch into a thriving business through a lot of hard work, striving to generate repeat business for years to come. It was amazing how she worked 7 days a week and 12-hour days for all those years. She loved the people that came through our gift shop door and was devoted to our deer.

I also want to mention our good friend Carolyn, who was an employee for all of the 23 years we owned the DEER RANCH. She was always there when we needed her, and being a farm girl, she was always willing to help with the deer.

John.3:3

Chapter 1 ~ Getting Started

My wife Sally and I got into the deer raising business in 1988 when we purchased a tourist attraction called the DEER RANCH in the tourist town of St. Ignace, Michigan from the former owner. St. Ignace is the gateway to the Upper Peninsula (UP) for those traveling north from Michigan's Lower Peninsula across the Mackinac Bridge on I-75, one of the state's major freeways. I-75 is not only one of the major north/south routes in Michigan, it extends from Canada all the way to Florida. The route funnels thousands of tourists to St. Ignace each summer from many states, not just those it goes through.

The major east/west route that brings tourists to St. Ignace is highway US 2. This scenic route borders the northern shore of Lake Michigan in places and extends as far west as Idaho. US 2 and I-75 intersect in St. Ignace, making this quaint northern town a major hub for travelers going through the UP regardless of which direction they are going.

Due to its prime geographic location, St. Ignace is one of the oldest cities in the United States. It was established in 1671. Sault Ste. Marie, Michigan and St. Augustine, Florida are the two cities that were founded before St. Ignace.

Since the entire UP is a tourist destination, it makes sense that one of the gateways to the region and one of its major hubs would cater to travelers looking for fun, entertainment and something exciting to do such as look at and photograph wildlife. That's why the DEER RANCH was established. It's located along US 2 five miles west of St. Ignace.

Sally and I were born and raised in St. Ignace and that's why we returned there during the summer of 1987. I'm a building contractor by trade. We had spent the previous three years in Lower Michigan, where I built five 60-unit motels for a friend. Once that job was done, we were ready to move back to our hometown.

That summer, Sally took a job in the gift shop at the DEER RANCH and ended up working with her best friend Joanne Tamlyn who had worked there for many years. By fall I told Sally that we needed to buy a gift shop or something to invest in for retirement as a carpenter only has a handful of nails and a few used tools to get rid of.

Word eventually spread to the owner of the DEER RANCH (Tom Harrington) that we were looking to invest in a local business. In the winter, he asked us if we were interested in buying his business, which consisted of the gift shop where Sally worked and live whitetail exhibit. I was interested, but the wife was worried if the investment would be worth it. So I had to convince Sally the investment was the right thing to do.

While still considering the purchase of the DEER RANCH, we made a trip to Berlin, Wisconsin where they made a lot of the deerskin products that were in the ranch's gift shop. While in that area, I took Sally to Wisconsin Dells where I found a giant leaping whitetail statue made out of fiberglass. That's what I needed to convince Sally we could make the DEER RANCH a success.

We could put a similar deer in front of the gift shop at the DEER RANCH as a way to get tourists to stop. I found the name of the company that made the deer statue at The Dells on the base of it and wrote it down so I could order one after we bought the DEER RANCH. That statue sealed the deal. With a giant deer to attract customers to our doors, how could we go wrong?

We took over the DEER RANCH on May 1, 1988. The next day, I called and ordered my big deer that was 14 feet high and 20 feet long. The company owner said the mold was at his mother-in-law's barn in storage, but he would dig it out.

That's how we became deer farmers, jumping into something new. I was a deer hunter for 25 years, so I did have a little understanding of whitetails, but it didn't take long to find out raising deer is different than hunting them.

One of the things I insisted on before buying the DEER RANCH from Tom Harrington is that he had to get two new bucks to replace the old ones. The bucks that were on exhibit were 10 and 12 years old and I knew they wouldn't last long. So when we took the business over, we had two young, healthy yearling bucks and 13 does in one large pen. The yearling bucks were obtained from the Renegade Ranch at Cheboygan.

Sally and I were the third owners of the DEER RANCH. The original owners were John and Irene Ogle. They had a gas station and grocery store and turned it into a gift shop and deer exhibit, naming it the DEER RANCH. The original deer that they put on exhibit in 1950 were buck and doe fawns that they got from a lady on the north side of town who was bottle feeding them. At the time, I don't think there were any laws about keeping wild animals.

Our food was a dry mix of oats, corn, barley, molasses and selenium that we got from a co-op 25 miles away, which was delivered in bulk, poured directly into our 3-ton silo. The former owner fed the deer every night at 5:00 p.m. and gave them water and hay. I knew I could do that without any difficulty.

Our large deer statue came in August. We mounted it on a large cube of concrete and we were ready for business. I was taking care of the deer, but Sally had the gift shop to run and she needed help. She called her friend Carolyn Dodson to ask her if she might be interested in a job as a clerk in the store.

"Would tomorrow be soon enough," Carolyn asked.

Wow, what luck. She had been helping her husband who was an undertaker and mayor in town and must have thought the DEER RANCH would be a good change. She ended up working for us for 23 years until we sold the place.

Seventeen fawns were born that first year. That was far too many for us to keep. So, that fall, we decided to sell the surplus. We didn't have a tranquilizing gun back then to use to capture the deer. The former owner of the DEER RANCH suggested that we close off the feed barn until morning. By then, the fawns would be the first to enter the barn to start eating.

He was right. After fawns entered the barn, I would shut the door on them, so they were trapped inside. From the barn, the fawns had to be chased into a chute that led to a trailer that they would be transported in. So after fawns were trapped in the feed barn, I entered the barn with them and had to try to chase them into the chute.

The fact that the mud was a foot deep complicated matters. Some of the fawns had other ideas, too. One jumped back over my head and knocked me in the mud and put a cut in my scalp with a sharp hoof. Right then I thought we have to find a better way for the future.

That fall I lost one of my nice new bucks due to blood poisoning. The veterinarian who examined him told me a thorn from a crabapple tree that had lodged in his leg got infected. She said with him so pumped up during the rut that there would have been no way to save him. Due to the loss of that buck, I had to replace him by the next spring.

Kaila out taking a sun bath in the flower patch

Chapter 2 ~ Changes Are Coming

With our first season at the DEER RANCH behind us and well on our way to learning how to be deer farmers, we needed some direction. One of the first things we had to do is locate a veterinarian we could depend on and establish a good relationship with them. We found a lady named Dr. Sara Michelin, D.V.M., who was a large animal veterinarian. At that time, no local veterinarians had much experience with whitetails. We would learn together and she could coach me on the medicines we needed to keep our deer healthy.

As a hunter, I knew that whitetails ate many times a day, so our feeding program had to be modified accordingly. I designed a four by four-foot plywood box with a smooth Masonite curved back so the feed would slide into a 12-inch by four-foot wide trough. It didn't take long for us to notice that the deer would go into the barn, where the feeder was located, eight or 10 times a day to eat a little food and then leave.

With only one buck left for our second season, we had to shop for another one. Ed's Archery in Clio, Michigan had a yearling that had his antlers injured from getting into the fence that they were willing to sell. We decided to buy that buck because the business owner (Ed Gilkes) told me he would replace him the next year if he didn't pan out. The yearling buck we got from Ed's Archery was named PEPI (Pep-pee). The whitetail had eight points the next year, so we kept him.

We named the buck BIG BOY that survived from our first year as owners of the DEER RANCH. I had built two Big Boy restaurants and thought that would be a good name. As time went on, he became our most photographed deer and lived up to his name.

At this stage as deer farmers, we realized that we needed some way to tranquilize the animals occasionally to handle them for a variety of reasons. Based on what we went through the year before to catch excess fawns to sell, we knew we had to do something different. We also needed a way to catch deer to treat those that became injured or sick like the buck we lost to blood poisoning and to give them medicine to help keep them healthy.

A tranquilizer gun is what we needed, and we ordered one. Such a gun is designed to shoot a hollow dart containing a safe drug like a sedative that causes deer to lie down once the drug is absorbed into their system. The drug doesn't put the animals to sleep, but they lose the ability to stand by relaxing their muscles.

The dosage of drug is varied depending upon the weight of the deer to be darted. Deer are usually darted in meaty areas such as the rump to reduce the chances of hurting them. Since whitetails are high strung, and this applies to captive whitetails as well as wild ones, using a dart gun to subdue them before handling them is easiest on the deer as well as deer farmers.

Back then, the drug we used in darts for the dart gun we purchased was Rompun. The drug would eventually wear off, but the process would take a long time. After we were done handling darted deer, the normal procedure was to administer a reversal drug with a syringe to counteract the Rompun. The reversal drug we used to counteract the effects of Rompun was Antagonal. Antagonal would get deer back on their feet fairly quickly after it was injected.

We could also use the tranquilizer gun to give medicine to deer without having to handle them. The medicine could be put in a dart instead of Rompun. The medicine would then be injected when the dart connected on the animal that needed it.

We also got a variety of "wormers" from Dr. Sara to reduce

the number of internal parasites in our deer. The wormer we used most often was Ivomec. Most dog owners are familiar with the value of using wormers on their pets to eliminate parasites. These types of preventative medicines are just as important for captive deer.

There was no deerfarmer.com and computers to go to for help back then, so we relied on a few other deer farmers and our veterinarian for advice. The deer farmers we knew were in the learning process, too.

With lots of tourist traffic and fawns being born, our second spring was proving to be a busy one. Early one morning, we were in for a surprise when a lady came out of our park and told us we had a fawn with a broken leg. It proved to be a three-day old fawn we named Betty. Her left rear leg was broken. We had to figure out what to do to help the injured fawn.

A call to the previous owner of the Deer Ranch didn't prove to be too helpful. His advice was to put the fawn down. I was not going to destroy that cute little fawn.

A call to the veterinarian clinic was next. After learning it would cost hundreds of dollars for x-rays and a cast for a $50 fawn, we ruled that out. As a deer farmer taking care of God's animals, I decided I would have to come up with a solution for the problem myself. I asked Sally to clear off the kitchen table so I could fix Betty's broken leg.

A couple of paint stirring sticks that were cut to fit served as splints for the leg. We set the rear leg bone back in place to the best of our ability and used tape to hold the splints in place. Once the operation was complete, we put the fawn back with her mom.

A week later, the sticks we used as splints were wearing down to the hoof. So I relied on my woodworking skills to fashion a new set of splints made out of more durable wood – oak. It's amazing how fast the little ones heal when they have the proper care. Three weeks later, we had to catch Betty to remove the oak splint, which was not easy. She had no difficulty eluding our efforts to catch her by then.

Lucky for me, I saw her sleeping in the roots of a big spruce tree one day. I was able to sneak up on the opposite side of the tree from where she was sleeping, then reached around the tree trunk and grabbed her. Betty was none too happy to be caught, however. I had all I could do to hang onto the kicking fawn. There's no way I could get my jackknife out of my pocket to cut the tape holding the splint in place. Fortunately, Sally showed up with a knife to cut the tape, so the splint could be removed.

Mom stimulating her fawn to go potty. The second reason mom is licking under the tail is she has to devour any waste. If any waste drops on the ground a predator would find the fawn so this is a safety factor to protect her fawn. Captive deer do this like wild deer for about 30 days or until a fawn can out run her predators.

When mom says wait your turn, she meant it!

Carpet, heated floors, what more could a fawn ask for!

Betty lived for many years and later gave birth to our first white whitetail. Her leg healed with a little turn to one side, but most people didn't notice it until you told them. Successfully treating Betty's broken leg is one of the things that made deer farming so rewarding.

Our only deer pen was 120 by 200-feet, so we decided to split it lengthwise. By forming two separate enclosures, we would be able to keep our two bucks apart, reducing the chances of them hurting each other. I don't know how the former owner kept two large bucks together without them killing one another. With PEPI getting bigger, we didn't want to take a chance of keeping him in with Big Boy.

We bought a white whitetail from a deer farmer in Pennsylvania that we thought would attract tourists to the Deer Ranch. We built a third pen for that deer. With new bucks we were able to keep a few fawns from our old stock for breeding purposes.

Chapter 3 ~ More Problems

Another spring is quickly approaching and we started to get excited about the fawns that we knew would soon arrive. We anticipated a good season since we were learning more and feeling confident about raising whitetails. We usually checked the deer and walked around the pen each day to make sure everything was okay before we let the public enter.

We were in for a surprise when we opened the gate one morning and found a doe that we thought was about to give birth to a fawn. Only two legs were sticking out. Upon closer examination, we determined the fawn was not moving and the legs were dry, indicating that it had been dead for a while. Checking a little closer, we realized it was the back legs that were protruding from the doe, resulting in a breech birth. Fawns are normally born headfirst.

Sally and I had to make a decision about what to do real fast. We did not want to tranquilize the doe for fear of also losing her. None of our 13 does in this pen were bottle fed, so they weren't used to being handled, but they were used to coming to the fence to eat food from the tourists. That gave us an idea of something to try.

I let Sally in the pen with crackers and I stayed outside. The doe must have sensed we were there to help her because Sally walked right up to her. As Sally talked to the doe and fed her crackers, my wife backed the deer toward me until I was able to grab the unborn fawn's legs. The doe pushed as I pulled and out came the fawn. That's another example of how Sally and I made a great team as deer farmers.

Since Betty, the doe that broke a hind leg when only three days old, was getting along very well without a limp, we had time to focus on the other does that I began to name. They

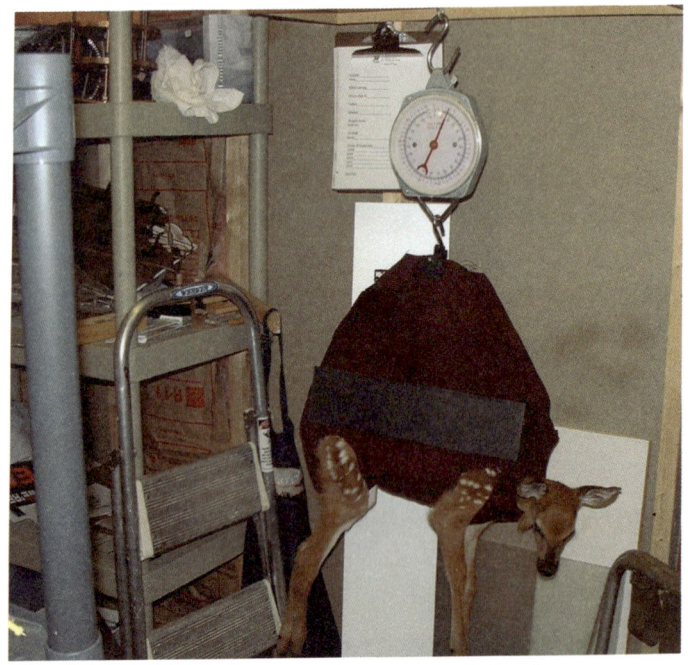

Home made fawn cradle, we weigh the fawns and give them their shots and ear tag.

Our smallest fawn ever weighing 3 pounds. So small it could not reach mom to nurse so had to be bottle fed

Hair Biting

We had a bottle-fed doe named Hina who started biting hair off of the other deer and herself. I moved her from pen to pen thinking it may have been one of the other deer causing her to do this. After moving her to the fifth pen with no change, we decided we would have to send her on her way.

By that time she had hardly any hair left on her body. Both of her sides were completely bare. She removed hair from where ever she could reach. Having a deer with little to no hair was not very appealing to the public. Not being able to determine why she was removing hair, we concluded that her hair biting was caused from nervousness like a human who constantly bites their fingernails.

were Goat Face, Horse Face, Wart, Bobtail and one with a bent nose we named Hook Nose. Looking at Betty's face and comparing her with other does, we figured the facial features that the other does exhibited might be from inbreeding over a period of years.

At that point, we decided it was time to start selling some of the older does and replace them with a fresh bloodline.

Fawning season came and left without many problems and we were able to finish the third pen along with a new barn while waiting for the white deer to arrive from Pennsylvania. Ed Gilkes from Ed's Archery in Clio, dropped the white buck off on his way to Wisconsin, where he was going to pick up some adult bucks. It was exciting getting our first white whitetail. He was a yearling that had been bottle-fed. The deer had brown eyes, was white as snow in color and very tame. We named him Sno-Flake due to how white he was. His coloration reminded us of snow.

On his return trip from Wisconsin, Ed dropped off a brown yearling that he picked up for us. We named him Wiskee and only kept him for a couple of years because his antlers didn't grow as large as we would have liked. He only grew nine point antlers after three years.

We also picked up a yearling buck from Traverse City that we named Bucky. That fall we decided to move Betty in with the white buck. Her coat was light colored, so we thought she would make the best mate for Sno-Flake. We hoped for the best from the pairing by the next spring.

Chapter 4 ~ Nature's Ways

As we started another season, we wondered what lie ahead for us. With six sets of twins on the ground and one set of triplets, it looked like we were off to a good start.

One of our 16-year-old does was giving birth to a fawn as I entered the park one day before we opened, which seemed normal. I continued walking around, counting heads and checking each pen, then went back to the old doe. She was lying motionless with the fawn next to her. I entered the pen and could hear no breathing and felt no heartbeat. A later autopsy revealed she had a heart attack.

With its mother out of the picture, the fawn needed immediate attention. A fawn's first meal is normally a special type of milk called colostrum that's a different consistency than regular milk. Colostrum is low in fat, but high in things that help kick start a fawn's system such as carbohydrates, protein and antibodies. Colostrum is easy for fawns to digest and contributes to keeping them healthy. This fawn needed colostrum.

I wrapped her in my jacket and headed for the gift shop. On the way to the gift shop, we noticed a doe in the next pen that was also giving birth. After putting the fawn in the gift shop where it would be safe, we headed back to watch the other doe that was giving birth. She was dropping her second fawn when we got back to her.

As we watched the doe cleaning the newborn by licking it, a thought came to Sally. Would that doe adopt the orphan? Back to the store I went and grabbed the little one. I then rushed into the pen with the newborn twins in an effort to find out the answer to Sally's question.

The new mom was still lying on the ground as I approached on my knees with the orphan. I was worried that she might get up and charge me to protect her fawns, but that didn't happen.

She moved away slowly, but kept an eye on me as I approached the twins. I had put rubber gloves on before I picked up the orphan, so I wouldn't get human scent on it. To make the doe think the orphan was one of her fawns, I rubbed afterbirth that resulted from birth of the twins, all over it. I then placed the orphan between the twins and left.

I went back to get a cup of coffee, then waited about 20 minutes before checking to see if I still had three fawns with the potential foster mother. It was a major relief to watch the doe nursing and licking all three fawns. She only had twins, but she raised all three that summer. She was a great foster mother.

Something that surprised us and that had never happened before, occurred about a week later. As I was giving shots to a two-day-old fawn, a two-week-old fawn came running up to me and started head butting me. I reached over and pushed on his forehead and he just kept on pushing. That little guy was only being nursed by its mother. We had not fed it from a bottle, so its human contact was limited.

That's why that fawn's behavior was so unusual. It showed no fear of me. Maybe because it saw me frequently and I occasionally interacted with other deer, the fawn thought I was part of the herd.

This behavior went on all summer when I went into his pen. He had no fear of humans and loved to play. Through the years we had a couple other fawns that acted similar to that one.

And I encountered a wild buck one time that seemed to have a similar attitude. Years ago, while out for a walk on an old logging trail, I came across a 4-point buck walking towards me. I stopped and he stopped 20 feet from me. It was close to the rut and I became a little nervous as he just stood there as I started talking to him. I reached into my pocket and pulled out my jackknife in case he came any closer. I hollered and he just walked around me with no fear whatsoever, keeping about 20 feet of distance between us.

Chapter 5 ~ Mother Nature Gets Our Fawns

Fall came and it was time to sell off the fawns produced that year since we would have more the next spring. Little did we know that we would need some of those fawns due to unexpected losses.

A fawns instinct is to crouch and be still.

Bronco and Nicole

Spring came, but the warmer temperature did not follow. Temperatures were as low as 22 degrees in the morning during May and June. With fawns born wet, and dropping on frozen ground, they were getting viral pneumonia and dying. Our veterinarian was supplying a poly serum to try to help save the sick fawns. I was averaging about a hundred shots a week to no avail.

Even with spreading straw around on the ground in the deer pens and in the barns, it didn't help much. The does would give birth wherever they wanted to when the time came. In many cases, it wasn't on the straw.

After losing more than a dozen fawns, our last pregnant doe was giving birth on the first warm day of the summer, which was June 26th. Our veterinarian suggested that if we wanted any fawns to survive that year we had better take them home to bottle-feed. The doe gave birth to twins, one fawn of each sex. We followed the doctor's suggestion and took them home with us. We named our house guests Jacob and Autumn.

They had the run of the house for about 50 days. While Jacob and Autumn were at the house, we constructed a fawn pen at the DEER RANCH to prepare for their return. After their stay at the house came to an end, we put them in the fawn pen that was ready and waiting for them.

That spring was the coldest ever recorded for our area and cost us a lot, but we had to lift our head high and move forward. It was another lesson about the challenges deer farmers face.

With fall approaching it was time to work on the deer pens. We decided to split pen number three lengthwise like we had done with pen number one.

When dealing with the public, we learned that all the deer had to look perfect or the customers would come back into the gift shop and complain to the clerks. We once had a lady come in to complain because there was a doe panting in the sun. She wanted us to make it go in the shade. We explained to the woman that the doe was no different than a human. The deer was simply sunbathing. The doe was free to get up anytime it wanted to and go under a tree or in the barn.

Then we would get complaints about all of our does abandoning their babies. Those people wanted us to do something about it. We did our best to explain to them that this is normal behavior among whitetails. It's a safety factor to reduce the chances of predators locating fawns. Even though does might not be by their fawns' sides, the mothers usually monitor the well being of their offspring from a safe distance.

Fawns are scent free from the time they are born until they are about 30 days old. This reduces the odds of predators finding fawns through their sense of smell. The spots on the coats of fawns are there for camouflage to reduce their visibility to predators when lying motionless on the forest floor. With this camouflage and no scent, a dog or coyote could walk right by them and never know they are there.

Since does do have plenty of scent and their larger size makes them more visible, they would attract attention to their fawns if the little ones were always with them. That would be a disadvantage before fawns are strong enough to outrun predators. By the time fawns are about four weeks of age, they are usually able to escape from predators.

The instinctive behavior both does and fawns exhibit during the fawns' first weeks of life proves GOD takes care of everything.

PEPI at age 2

PEPI during Rut

Chapter 6 ~ PEPI

Chapter two tells about getting PEPI (pronounced PEP-PEE). That buck represented our first purchase of new bloodlines.

Pepi was born on June 28, 1988. He came to us in the fall of 1989 with deformed antlers caused by tangling with a fence. The next year he was a nice 8-pointer. Since he was bottle-fed as a fawn, he was dog tame. You will find a list in this chapter of the antlers he grew during the 12 years of his life.

The age he attained is ancient for whitetail bucks. Although a few wild whitetails make it to 10 years of age, and some of the bucks bagged by hunters in the UP have gotten that old, most bucks living in the wild seldom reach five years old. The annual breeding season and the associated stress, is rough on adult bucks.

We mounted PEPI's antlers so tourists could see them.

Fights between bucks are common and they sometimes injure or kill one another. Their antlers occasionally lock together during fights, and if no one rescues them in time, both bucks die. Bucks also suffer accidents during the many miles they travel in search of does, often getting hit by vehicles as they attempt to cross roads.

Bucks also lose up to 25 percent of their weight during the breeding season and that weight loss makes them vulnerable to predators. Severe winters also claim plenty of bucks that have lost their fat reserves during the breeding season.

Whitetail bucks grow a new set of antlers every year. The new antlers usually start growing in April. The growing antlers are covered with tissue that is soft and covered with short hairs that is called velvet. Antler growth is normally complete by September. Most bucks shed the velvet covering on their antlers some time during the first half of that month.

Bucks rub their antlers on saplings, brush and trees to get rid of the velvet from their headgear. Some bucks may shed the velvet from their antlers in an hour, and others take all day. Once the velvet is gone, the antlers are solid bone.

Adult bucks will continue to rub their antlers on saplings and trees, especially during the breeding season or rut, to leave territorial markers and as a means of strengthening neck muscles for possible battles for dominance with other bucks. Not all fights between bucks are serious. Many bucks routinely engage in playful sparring matches to practice for the real thing.

Here's the list of PEPI's antler development. During the first six years of PEPI's life he grew typical antlers. After that, he grew nontypical drop tines.

1989 - injured spikes
1990 - 8 points
1991 - 10 points

1992 – 11 points
1993 – 11 points
1994 – 9 points, 1 drop tine
1995 – 11 points, 2 drop tines
1996 – 11 points, 3 drop tines
1997 – 11 points, 3 drop tines
1998 - 11 points, 3 drop tines
1999 – 11 points, 3 drop tines
2000 – at age 12 Pepi dropped to 8 points

PEPI's antler development during 1994 clearly shows the impact weather can have on the growth of antlers. He grew 11 points during 1992 and 1993, but only grew 9 typical points and one drop tine during 1994. He went back to growing 11 typical points from 1995 through 1999.

The reason PEPI only had 9 points in 1994 is that summer was much colder than normal. Most days were cloudy. There wasn't much sunshine that summer. With a hot summer and good sunshine, antlers will grow one-half to one-inch a day, making them the fastest growing tissue in the world.

The older bucks get, the better the chances they will grow nontypical points. PEPI's antler development during the course of his life follows that pattern. He grew his first drop tine when he was six years old, added another one the following year and developed three nontypical points over a span of four years starting at age eight.

The antlers of really old bucks start going downhill in size, and PEPI was definitely an oldtimer when he reached 12 years of age. That's when he only grew 8 points, the same as when he was two.

Bucks start losing their antlers in Michigan during December, but those that are in good condition sometimes retain their antlers until March or April. Since captive deer aren't often as nutritionally stressed as those in the wild, they will often keep their antlers longer than wild bucks.

Here are the dates by year that PEPI lost his antlers.

Year	Date
1992	2/27
1993	2/12
1994	2/10
1995	2/9
1996	1/31
1997	2/5
1998	2/1
1999	1/28

As you can see, this buck lost his antlers most often during February, but they fell off toward the end of January in 1996 and 1999.

If it weren't for an injury that PEPI suffered during the fall of 2000, he might have lived years longer. One day during that fall we noticed PEPI's jaw didn't look normal. It looked like his jaw might be broken, so we called our veterinarian to have a look at him.

Chapter 17 tells about moving Brandi by myself. This is my home made cart I used. Move the handle to the side and slide a deer right in. Great for moving deer by yourself.

Bronco shedding velvet in August

Dr. Sara said his jaw was indeed broken. She said the injury was not repairable, preventing the buck from being able to eat. So the broken jaw sealed his fate. After having that buck for 12 years, there was no way I could put him down.ABr. Sara did what had to be done. She gave PEPI a shot, putting him to sleep painlessly.

How did PEPI break his jaw? Coyotes and dogs are occasionally attracted to the deer pens. When that happens, the deer panic and they sometimes hurt themselves by running into the fence. But none of the does had a hair out of place, which ruled out coyotes or dogs as the reason behind PEPI's injury. The does would have showed signs of stress, too, if canines had disrupted the deer.

Some time later, as I walked around the outside of PEPI's pen, I found the answer to the questions of how and why he managed to break his jaw. A wild buck was responsible. Lying on the ground outside the pen near the fence was an antler with six points. PEPI instinctively tried to fight with a wild 12-point buck through the fence to protect his does from the strange buck. While doing so, he must have broken his jaw.

Chapter 7 ~ Big Boy Shines

Over the years, we have met a lot of people at the DEER RANCH, but one guy always showed up to photograph our deer. His name is Larry Cory and he does wildlife paintings. Larry attends lots of shows to display and sell his work. He loved Big Boy and took lots of pictures of him. He commented that Big Boy is one of the most photogenic deer he has ever photographed.

Larry entered one of the photos he took of Big Boy in the 1995 Purina Mills calendar shoot and his photo of Big Boy was picked for the cover.

The following year, Larry entered a painting of Big Boy in the Michigan United Conversation Clubs (MUCC) Christmas art contest. The painting of Big Boy did not win, but MUCC was so impressed with the painting that they picked it for use on their Christmas cards for 1996. The painting shows Big Boy standing near a stream that runs through Larry's property.

Not long after the painting of Big Boy was selected for MUCC's Christmas cards, the buck's life came to an end. In January of 1997, as the rut was coming to an end, Big Boy suffered a massive heart attack at the age of 10. An autopsy was performed to determine the cause of death. It was determined that Big Boy had scar tissue on his heart and lungs, which contributed to his untimely death. The veterinarian who examined him said it looked like Big Boy was born with this condition.

That might explain why Big Boy was always calm during the rutting season. He never charged the fence that separated his pen from the enclosure occupied by the buck next door in an effort to fight with him. Most other antlered whitetails that we owned usually tried to fight with neighboring bucks during the rut even though the fence was in the way of that happening. If they could see another buck, they tried to engage them in battle.

The largest set of antlers Big Boy grew during his life had 10 points. He usually carried his antlers well into March. Here are the dates by year when he lost his antlers, starting with 1992.

Our Postcard of Big Boy

1992 3/20
1993 3/12
1994 3/22
1995 3/18
1996 2/13
1997 Died on 1/11

When Big Boy was nine years old, he lost his antlers more than a month earlier than normal. The winter of 1995-1996 was a record tough one, with consistent snow cover starting during early November. There was also record snowfall and cold temperatures.

So winter weather probably contributed to the early antler drop. The fact that Pepi also lost his antlers earlier than normal that year (Chapter 6) helps confirm that. But Big Boy's declining health may have been a contributing factor to early antler loss, too.

I often found myself pondering why we lose deer. At those times, a thought a cow farmer shared with me invariably comes to mind.

"Harold you have to realize that the animals are God's creatures," he told me, "and you are just the caretaker doing the best you can with what you have."

I figured from then on we would have to harden our hearts to be deer farmers. This was not easy for Sally, especially at times when we lost fawns. I remember one time when she was holding a sick fawn as I gave it a shot to try to help it recover. Tears were streaming down her cheeks as the fawn expired in her lap. That type of thing would be hard on anyone.

There are ups and downs that come with being a deer farmer, just like many other things in life. Fortunately, the ups outweigh the downs, especially when we were lucky enough to witness the birth of fawns or observe antlers growing up to half an inch on a daily basis.

Chapter 8 ~ Learning the Hard Way

One spring the Michigan Deer Breeders held a meeting in Clare, Michigan. We decided to attend and set up a couple of tables to sell deer skin products that we stocked in our gift shop. The meeting was informative and we sold a lot of products to start out the season. We also got to meet a lot of deer breeders.

We learned a number of things about raising deer while talking to the breeders. One of the things we learned that proved valuable is the options for feeding our deer.

For the previous nine years we were getting our deer food mixed at the local co-op. At the time, little did we know that was about to change. The death of a newborn fawn for no apparent reason is what started the wheels turning toward a change. A necropsy revealed the fawn died from selenium toxicity.

We wondered how that could happen since Michigan has no selenium in the soil. We give newborns selenium at birth, but only in dosages of ¼ cc. I knew I couldn›t have overdosed the fawn, so it came down to the food its mother ate. Upon checking, we found out that the co-op was mixing six pounds of selenium per three tons of feed. Our veterinarian and co-op figured the selenium was damp and never mixed properly with the food in the 54-grind mixer they were using. Due to the fact the selenium was not properly mixed with the food we had, the fawn's mother consumed too much selenium and passed it on to the fawn through milk the doe was producing.

That doe did survive, but she lost her only fawn that year. From that day on we switched to commercial pellets designed for feeding deer, so we would not ever have that kind of trouble again. As we would find out later, there can be problems with pellets, too. At one point, we had to get rid of three tons of pellets. I will tell you why in the last chapter of this book.

The previous fall, we bred Jacob, our bottle-fed buck, to a white whitetail doe named Kaitlin. We were in for a big surprise when Kaitlin gave birth. Everything that I read about piebald deer said that you had to have two piebald parents to get a piebald fawn.

Kaitlin and her twins, One brown and one piebald

Piebalds are whitetails that have more white coloration than normal. The amount of extra white coloration that piebalds have can vary widely. The added white can be anything from a few spots to almost totally white.

If you guessed that Kaitlin gave birth to a piebald fawn, you would be right. She had two buck fawns, one of which was a piebald and the twin was normal in coloration. The partially white fawn that Kaitlin had proved that everything I read previously about what it takes to produce piebald offspring was wrong.

Earlier in the spring, I had put black shade cloth against Jacob's fence so he would not see the white buck in the adjoining pen. The cloth served the purpose it was intended for, but putting the cloth on the inside of the fence where the deer were, turned out to be a bad choice. I arrived at the DEER RANCH early one morning to find Jacob tangled in the shade cloth. Since he was tame from us bottle feeding him, I thought I would be able to go up to him, cut the cloth and untangle him.

That was another mistake. As I tried to untangle him, he tore away an eight-foot piece of cloth and went running from one end of the pen to the other, spooking all of the deer with the shade cloth that he had on him. Whitetails are easily spooked by anything they are unfamiliar with. And deer are good at spooking one another. If one is scared and starts running, the others usually follow suit.

Jacob charging around draped in shade cloth was a double

Save a lot of paper towels but they don't always hit the jar. This is Sierra. Notice the hair loss around the tail and back legs from bad milk replacer mentioned in chapter 18.

whammy. Who knows what the other deer thought he was. Perhaps they thought the shade cloth had attacked him and he was trying to get rid of it. The buck was obviously trying to get rid of the cloth, but he created pandemonium in the process.

The next move on my part was to tranquilize Jacob and the piebald fawn so they wouldn't get hurt. Fortunately, the white doe remained calm through the entire ordeal. After things settled down and I thought the deer were sleeping, it was time for me to move in with the dart gun.

When I got to Jacob, however, he was not sleeping. He was lifeless, with no heartbeat. His heart must have given out from the excitement. Checking the piebald fawn, I found the same situation. He was also dead. I should have taken that fawn home to bottle-feed him.

I was already bottle-feeding two fawns, however, and decided to let Kaitlin take care of her fawns. This was a costly mistake to learn. It's important to always put shade cloth on the outside of the fence, where it's used. We also installed a double fence between pens, which has worked well. The double fencing is four feet apart, providing a place to plant trees. The planted trees serve as a screen between pens and the trees planted in those locations can't be destroyed by bucks wanting to rub their antlers because bucks can't get at them.

Jacob was eight years old when he died. He was an average buck in terms of antler growth. He never grew more than 8 points on his antlers. Most bucks never do, of course. Eight is the most common number of antler points grown by adult bucks in North America.

What's real interesting about Jacob is he lost his antlers on the same date seven years in a row. That date was April 15, the same day income tax returns are due each year for residents of the United States.

Chapter 9 ~ World's Oldest Whitetail

The DEER RANCH was home to what is believed to be the world's oldest whitetail. That deer was a doe named Elizabeth. She was born on June 3, 1977 and she died on January 27, 2002. She lived to be 24 years and 7 months old.

Elizabeth may have also set records for the oldest doe to produce fawns and the number of fawns she had. According to the Michigan Department of Natural Resources (DNR), the oldest doe known to give birth was 13 years of age. Few does even reach that age. Elizabeth was still having fawns well beyond 13. In fact, she had fawns during every year of her life, including one year she was given birth control to try to prevent her from becoming pregnant.

Elizabeth was 11 years old when we bought the DEER RANCH, which is old by whitetail standards. At the time, we had no idea that she would go on to set such amazing records. This old doe produced 38 fawns during her lifetime, including twin females born on May 17, 2001.

Elizabeth didn't have her first fawn until she was two years old in 1979. She had a single fawn that year. Starting in 1980, she consistently produced twins every year through 1990, except in 1988, when she gave birth to a single fawn. Through 1989, at the age of 12, the doe had produced a total of 20 fawns. She almost doubled that figure by the time she reached 24 in 2001 even though she gave birth to single fawns six of those years. From 1991 through 1997 Elizabeth dropped single fawns each year, except 1993 when she had twins. If the doe would have lived five months longer, she would have doubled her output of fawns.

In July of 1997, Elizabeth lost the lone fawn she had that year due to the lack of colostrum in her milk. The following fall (1998), we decided to give her the birth control drug Latalyse in an effort to prevent her from having any more fawns because of her advanced age. We figured the drug would prevent her from getting pregnant and make life easier on the old deer by reducing the drain associated with fawn production.

Latalyse had worked well for us when we used it on doe fawns that we left with bucks during the breeding season. Without some type of birth control, many doe fawns come into heat at the age of six months and would have a single fawn in September. That's too late for fawns to be born in our northern climate because they would not have time to grow a winter coat before winter arrived. By using Latalyse to prevent doe fawns from coming into heat, most of our does were 18 months old before they bred for the first time and had their first fawns at two years of age.

In spite of our efforts to prevent Elizabeth from getting pregnant during the fall of 1998, she got pregnant anyway. We were still surprised when, during the spring of 1999, she seemed to be gaining weight and was starting to look pregnant. Based on our years of experience watching pregnant does, we noticed that they would pace back and forth along the fence about a day before giving birth. Well, Elizabeth was pacing on May 23rd and the next day she gave birth to twins at 22 years of age. There was a fawn of each sex. These were fawn number 33 and 34 for Elizabeth.

Since I flunked birth control class with Elizabeth, I decided to let nature take its course after that. She had twins again during 2000 and 2001 and would have had two more in 2002, if she would have lived long enough.

Of the six sets of twins Elizabeth had given birth to since 1990, two sets were females, two were males and two were one of each sex. Four out of the six single fawns the doe had were bucks.

Elizabeth with her single number 34 fawn with more to come

Birthing dates for Elizabeth since 1990 clearly show that she was bred at different times most years, although her advanced age might have had something to do with that. In 1990, for instance, her fawns were born on May 23. The following year, they were born a month later on June 23. During 1992, she gave birth on June 1 and in 1993 she dropped a fawn on July 21.

This special doe had fawns more often during late May, however, than in June or July. During 1999, for example, she dropped her fawns on May 24 and had them on May 25 during 1998. The birth date for her fawns in 1995 was May 26. Since there's roughly a seven-month gestation period for whitetails, Elizabeth was bred most often during late October.

Wild whitetails seldom exceed 10 years of age, but a few deer of both sexes do manage to live longer than normal. Does have a better chance of reaching older age than bucks because they don't endure the stress associated with the rut. Deer without antlers are also more likely to be passed up by hunters. The oldest doe taken by a hunter in Michigan was an amazing 19.5 years old. That doe was shot during the 1967 hunting season and her age was determined from her teeth. Does that were 14.5 and 15.5 years of age have also been taken by hunters.

I'm sure Elizabeth will be missed at the DEER RANCH, as she was a very productive member of the family. We saved her lower jawbone with all of her teeth still in place so we could have it aged without telling anyone her real age. This would be a way to check their accuracy. So far we have not found the right people to do this with.

Chapter 10 ~ Long Toenails & Skinny Does

Deer can groom themselves, but we still had to do regular maintenance and care along with responding to accidents that happened. Over the years, we have had many different things we learned about caring for our deer. And for serious problems, we had to rely on our veterinarian. This chapter deals with a couple of the problems we faced.

Another couple who were raising deer about 35 miles south of us contacted us about buying two fawns after they were weaned. One of the fawns was a buck we did not need, but we figured we could sell him with our other fawns in the fall. The doe fawn would provide a new bloodline to add to our herd. We thought it was a good idea at the time, but making the decision to add that doe to our herd turned out to be a mistake.

We named that doe Lacy. It didn't take long to find out that she had excessive toenail (hoof) growth unlike any of our other deer. Our window for trimming nails (hooves) was very short. After March 1st we would not tranquilize a doe for fear the drugs could cause a pregnant doe to abort her fawn. During the summer, we worried about tranquilizing a nursing doe for fear of the drugs affecting her milk.

Our window of opportunity to provide care for does that required tranquilizing them was September through April. Our problem arose during the summer as Lacy's hooves really grew and we had the public coming in every day. By September, her hooves were four inches long. We trimmed them in the fall and then again on the first of March.

Our five deer pens had a lot of gravel on the ground, which helped the other deers' hooves wear down, but not Lacy's.

We decided that after the second year of dealing with Lacy's hooves, we would pass her on to another farm that did not have their deer on exhibit to the public. We also sold all of her fawns, so we could get rid of this genetic trait.

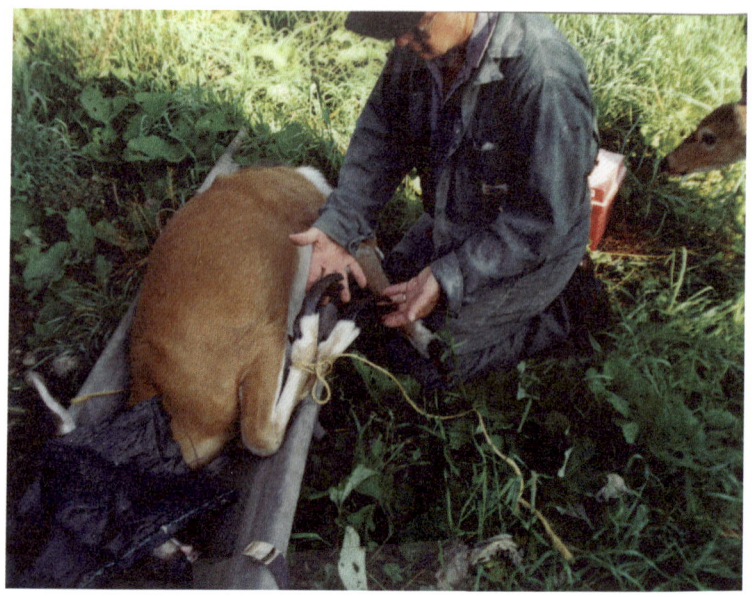

Lacy at the nail salon

Early summer was also a time that the does looked their worst, with some of their old dead winter hair holding on, and the red summer coat taking forever to come in. The bucks would get their summer coat early because stress was minimal for them at that time of year. The only thing bucks had going was growing antlers. Their antlers could grow up to one inch a day, which is the fastest growing living tissue in the world.

That time of year is stressful for does because all of their energy is going into final development of the fawns inside of them and the process of making milk to prepare for birth of the fawns. That leaves growth of their summer coat on the back burner. And once fawns are born, does are constantly nursing their offspring, which prevents them from gaining weight. They may even lose weight while caring for their fawns, making them look skinny. Does that have triplets experience the greatest drain.

When does are nursing their fawns it's common to see their ribs and a lot of people ask if we are feeding them. When we got this question, we told our visitors that all five pens had a feed box containing 900 pounds of pellets in front of them at all times. Our deer normally ate a handful of pellets eight or nine times a day. They only ate what they needed. They never overate. By fall, the does gained weight, and then got pregnant, starting the cycle all over again.

Brief Whitetail Facts

- Male deer may be called buck, bulls, stags, or harts
- Female deer may be called does, cows, or hinds
- Young deer are know as fawns or calfs
- Deer are ruminants, also know as cud chewers
- Scientifically they are part of the family Cervidae, order Artiodactyle
- Top running speed of a whitetail (40 mph)
- Top swimming speed of a whitetail (13 mph)
- Average tail length of a whitetail (10.6 inches)
- Average number of pounds of vegetation a whitetail will consume in a single day (7)
- Number of stomachs a whitetail has (4)

Chapter 11 ~ Tail Biting

This is a story about does biting off the tails of their fawns. Bunnies with antlers is fiction. Whitetails with bunny tails is a fact.

After 12 years of raising whitetails, you start to feel confident in yourself and your knowledge about deer. You think you know it all. That's when the deer have a tendency to prove otherwise.

When we purchased the DEER RANCH, there were about 15 deer present. Some appeared to be inbred. One was a runt doe that had a very short tail about an inch long. After we took over, we started to replace all the old stock with new bloodlines. We kept two of the original does. One was Elizabeth because she was the oldest. The other was Bob-tail because she was very friendly and was the first to come to the fence for a cracker or piece of carrot. We figured the short tail was from inbreeding and would never happen again with new stock.

Bob-tail lived with us for seven years and produced many normal fawns before she died.

A couple of years later, we had a fawn born that had a bloody tail after it was a week old. Closer examination showed most of the tail was gone. A few stitches and a little iodine fixed her right up, but the mystery remained about what happened to the fawn's tail. Maybe a weasel or coon had nipped it off or a larger deer stepped on it with a sharp hoof. We didn't know why, but we had a deer with a bunny tail. The name we gave that fawn at birth was Erin, but we changed it to Bob-tail from that day on since the original Bob-tail was no longer with us.

Another two years went by before we had some answers to the mystery about what happened to the newborn's tail. A white whitetail doe named Kaitlin would shed some light on this mystery when she gave birth to a white doe fawn we named Lucy. About six days after Lucy was born, my wife and I were strolling through the park and stopped to watch Kaitlin nursing Lucy.

Everything looked normal as Kaitlin was licking under the tail of her fawn as the youngster nursed. But then the mother started to chew the white fawn's tail off. We hollered to try to stop the doe, but the damage was done. Another suture and iodine treatment took care of the tail injury. That time we knew how the fawn's tail was damaged, and how we came to have another bunny-tailed deer.

We had the who and how surrounding the shortened tails, but not the why to this mystery. A brown doe named Fawnee that we bottle-fed was the next deer to provide us with information on the subject after she had triplets. All three fawns were females. One day we witnessed Fawnee bite off the tail of one of her fawns just like Kaitlin had done. The doe only bit off the tail of one fawn. Why would she target only one fawn to treat that way and not touch the other two?

We are still pondering the answer to that question. We do not know why a doe would damage any of her offspring's tails.

With three does that had bunny tails at that point, we were wondering what surprise would be in store for the following year. We usually sell our excess fawns in the fall, but nobody wants a whitetail without a tail, so we were stuck with the bunny-tailed deer. I'm sure some big, brown-eyed doe will test my knowledge about deer again in the future.

Chapter 12 ~ Harden Your Heart

The year of 2008 started out as a normal year until August 28th arrived. One of the deer at a Lower Michigan deer farm near Grand Rapids was found to have chronic wasting disease (CWD). The diseased deer was a three-year-old doe that had been bottle-fed. This development would affect all deer farmers in Michigan with a quarantine. No movement of any deer in or out from captive deer facilities was permitted.

Caroline and her favorite doe Fawnee

Every day, a conservation officer was at our DEER RANCH, checking to see that no deer moved in or out. If a fawn died, it had to be buried in that pen.

This had us worried because every September we sold our excess fawns to make room for the new batch of fawns the following year. By the middle of September, and we had 17 fawns to get rid of, with no buyers in sight. Each deer farmer had his own whitetails to worry about. The quarantine was finally lifted on September 22nd because we were certified

CWD-free since 2002. We achieved that status before many other farms.

We made lots of phone calls to try to sell our fawns after the quarantine was lifted, but had no luck in finding a buyer until placing a call to a Flint area breeder that we had sold fawns to before. He was interested in purchasing our fawns. We settled on a price of $100 apiece, but his partner backed out of the deal, claiming they would not be able to afford the food to feed the fawns.

I then dropped the price to $50 apiece for the fawns, but got the same answer. The next offer was all 17 fawns free, just to get rid of them, so we would have room for more, but they still passed.

We made more phone calls to as many breeders as we could think of, but everybody was still under the quarantine. So they couldn't buy the fawns even if they wanted to. I thought about releasing the fawns into the wild, but that was also illegal. That brought us to a decision we did not want to ever face. We would have to euthanize all of our fawns.

We would need help, so we turned to Trooper Fred Strich, a Michigan State Police Trooper who became the Drug Abuse Resistance Education (DARE) Officer in local schools when he was transferred to St. Ignace. Sally and I had been involved with the DARE program since 1989. Our DEER RANCH would supply one large Dare Bear to each of the five classes in Mackinac County. After going to a couple of DARE graduations, we decided to supply a small Dare Bear to every child in the county that graduated. Our greatest reward was when a mother who told us her daughter was off to college with her little Dare Bear in tow.

We wanted to donate the meat from the fawns we euthanized to needy families, so we could not use a tranquilizing drug. Nor did we want to use a loud gun that would spook the other deer. We decided to use a .22 caliber rimfire rifle, shooting .22 shorts. Those bullets made close to the same amount of noise as our tranquilizer gun.

We planned to place the shots so the young deer would drop instantly and not spook the other whitetails. Everything went as planned. We took eight fawns the first day and nine the next day. Most of the meat was given to the Legacy House for battered women. Even though the meat was put to good use, killing those fawns was the hardest thing we ever had to do as deer farmers.

Loss of a Doe

In Chapter 11 we told you about Fawnee biting off the tail of one of her triplets. We bottle-fed Fawnee in 1994. She was the third fawn we had in our house. Fawnee didn't have a fawn until 1998. During 2006, we put her in with a bottle-fed buck named Bronco. At 12-years-old then, she was overweight and had arthritis

in her knees. She had a tough time getting around. When she moved, she moved slowly.

In November we were working around the pens when Sally noticed Bronco had blood and hair on his antlers. Worried about Fawnee's welfare, she told me to go to the pen Bronco was in to see what was going on. I rushed over there to find all of the does standing, except Fawnee. She was hiding in the far corner of the pen.

There was no way I was going to go in that pen with Bronco present. Bucks get aggressive during the breeding season due to high levels of testosterone and they can be dangerous. The fact that Bronco had blood on his antlers was proof enough that he was dangerous. Plenty of people have been injured or killed by captive rutting bucks. I didn't want to be added to the list.

To make it safe for me to go in the pen, I put Bronco down for a short nap. Once he went down, I proceeded to check on

Fawnee. She was lying down when I got to her, so I helped her get up and then examined her for any injury. I didn't see any blood or damage, so I thought she was okay.

I then decided I had to get Fawnee outside of the pen to reduce the chances of the buck hurting her. As I helped her walk out of the pen, however, I heard the sound of air coming out of her side. Unfortunately, Bronco had punctured her chest cavity, putting a small hole in a lung. The buck probably stabbed her while trying to get her up.

Sally asked if I was going to cut off Bronco's antlers while he was tranquilized. I didn't think that was necessary because I thought him injuring Fawnee was just an accident. As I laid Fawnee down outside the pen she had been in, she took her last breath. Her death brought a tear to our eyes. That was like losing a family member.

As it turned out, I should have cut Bronco's antlers off while I had him down, as Sally asked me to. In February he killed another doe with his antlers. That doe had not been bottle-fed like Fawnee, so we weren't as close to her, but she still represented a loss that could have been prevented.

Even though the rut was over when Bronco killed the second doe, I still would not take a chance on going in the pen with him. We put him down, so I could deal with the dead doe, and this time we cut the antlers off before we administered the reversal drug.

We never figured out why Bronco killed two does. He never hurt another doe and he was still living when we sold the DEER RANCH.

Chapter 13 ~ TB Testing

Tuberculosis or TB, as the disease is frequently called, created more paperwork for Michigan deer farmers. A hunter in the northeastern Lower Peninsula's Alcona County took the first whitetail in the state known to have TB during 1975. It was a 9 ½-year-old doe. At the time, the DNR thought it was an isolated case and nothing to worry about.

But when a second deer with the disease surfaced during 1994 in Alpena County, only eight miles from where the first TB positive whitetail came from, the DNR looked at the situation more seriously. The second diseased deer was a 4 ½-year-old buck. Once the DNR started testing deer for the disease, it didn't take long for more cases, hundreds of them, to be confirmed.

Although most of the diseased deer came from Alcona and Alpena Counties, whitetails that tested positive for TB came from six adjoining counties, too. Once the DNR realized the extent of the problem, they began requiring testing of captive deer, with deer farmers required to keep paperwork showing the results of testing on their animals.

Rules that required deer farmers and breeders to have their animals tested went into effect during 2000. The year before those rules took effect, members of the Michigan Deer Breeders Association decided to start testing to get a jump on the process.

We started our TB testing on October 18, 1999. Dr. Sara was approved by the state to do TB testing. When that morning arrived, we had Bill Van de Bogart from Traverse City with us, who is also a deer farmer, to help out if problems developed with my dart gun. The deer would have to be tranquilized to be tested. It's nice to have two shooters to get the job done quicker.

I was as nervous as a dog pooping razor blades. We had four deer pens holding a total of 22 deer. That's a lot of deer handling and I didn't want anything to go wrong. I didn't want any of the deer to get hurt and I certainly didn't want any of them testing positive for TB, although I was confident none of the whitetails at the DEER RANCH had the disease. There was a buck and four or five does in each pen. Once deer were tranquilized, Dr. Sara shaved their necks for the TB test, which required an injection. It was important to be able to see if there was any skin reaction to the injection. That's why the site of the injection had to be shaved.

At the same time Dr. Sara was administering the TB test, I gave each deer a wormer, checked their ear tags and hooves to see if they needed trimming. After all of the handling was done, we gave the does a reversal drug first. Then, after they were up on their feet, we would give the buck the reversal drug.

Everything went well until we got to pen four. A doe in that pen seemed to be out and ready for examination, until I knelt down to check her back toenails. The muscle relaxant hadn't totally taken effect yet because the doe suddenly kicked me in the chest, knocking me up against a tree. That was the last thing she did before going to sleep. I ended up with a cracked sternum from that unexpected, but powerful kick.

We were required to do TB testing for three years in a row and then every three years, even though no deer with TB have been detected in the UP. For that reason, the UP is designated as a TB Free Zone by the Department of Agriculture.

Three days or seventy hours after the TB test was originally administered, we had to sedate all of the deer again so Dr. Sara could feel the injection for any reaction. Our deer always tested negative.

When TB testing our deer a few years later, I told Dr. Sara I had a doe I wanted to move to a different pen. The reason for moving the doe is she never got pregnant from the buck she had been with for three years. This doe's name was Brandi. When Dr. Sara was examining her she called me over to explain why Brandi hadn't gotten pregnant.

"Feel down here," she instructed me while showing where she meant with her hands.

There were testicles present under the "doe's" skin. We put Brandi in a pen with a different buck, but we didn't expect anything to come of it. Brandi got her name changed to "IT." That wasn't the last surprise that unique doe gave us. In chapter 17 you will read how the former Brandi gave birth to a freak of nature.

During one of our TB test sessions, we decided not to put the bottle-fed buck down to feel his neck because I didn't think it was necessary. Since we had bottle-fed the buck and he was used to being handled by people, I figured we could feel his neck with him awake. We didn't consider the danger the buck posed to the four does in the same pen that we did tranquilize.

This could have been a costly mistake. As one of the does was coming to after the reversal drug had been injected, she staggered against the fence and the buck was right there to gore her. Fortunately, we were able to distract the buck long enough for her to shake out the cobwebs and regain her balance. From then on we sedated all the bucks and they weren't given the reversal drug until after all of doe's were standing.

The deer in pen five were the last to be TB tested. One of the deer in that pen, a doe named AMY, was always slow to go down after being sedated. I had darted her twice, so I figured she had enough drug this time. When I approached her, I straddled her back to put a hood over her nose to slide in place over her eyes. As I did that, the doe reared up and the back of her head smacked me in the nose.

Like the doe that kicked me, that was the last thing AMY

did before the drug finally took effect. After hitting me with her head, AMY laid down and never moved again until we gave her the reversal drug. I was a bloody mess with a broken nose, but we had to finish. I was glad she was the last one in that pen to do.

The day before another TB test was going to be conducted on our deer, one of the does was having a hard time breathing. So I gave the doe a shot to help her condition, and planned on having the veterinarian look at the deer the following day. After that doe was sedated the next day, Dr. Sara said it sounded like the deer had pneumonia. As the doctor was shaving the doe's neck, the doe quit breathing.

Dr. Sara told me to hold the doe's head up as the veterinarian did chest compressions. That got the doe breathing again. Then we gave the deer a reversal drug and got her on her feet. The doe was fine after that, with no further problems.

Three days later, I came down with pneumonia and I might have gotten it from the doe. I did not have gloves on as I was holding the doe's head up and her tongue was hanging out. I could have contracted pneumonia from her.

Over the years, we TB tested our deer six times. Since the deer had to be sedated twice for each test, once when they were inoculated and then again to test the results, each animal was sedated a total of 12 times. During all of that testing, there wasn't a single mishap to any of the deer. Although, as mentioned earlier, I wasn't as lucky.

Some deer farmers and breeders use a squeeze chute to hold whitetails for testing instead of sedating them, but I've heard too many stories about whitetails suffering broken legs from that method. So we continued to use a dart gun to put deer down for testing. That method has proven 100 percent safe for the deer, but not always for the deer farmer.

Chapter 14 ~ Deer Whisperer Gets His Name

Having a roadside tourist attraction exhibiting whitetails resulted in many people bringing us plenty of fawns that they found. State law prohibits us from taking any wild deer. Our deer are TB and chronic wasting disease (CWD) free. Our deer are also given a high protein pellet diet as well as the best of medicine and wormer available to keep them healthy. Bringing a wild fawn into our farm could infect our deer with a disease or parasites.

Sally & Harold with new twins

While it's illegal for us to add wild deer to our herd, it's also illegal for anyone to remove fawns from the wild. Most fawns that are "found" are not orphans. They are simply lying motionless where their mother left them, relying on their natural camouflage to go undetected. Although most people who try to "rescue" fawns don't know it, the youngster's mother is usually nearby watching them just out of view. Besides being illegal, removing fawns from the wild and their mother's care reduces their chances of survival.

One day we had a salesman wearing a suit and tie bring twin fawns to us that he said he found alongside the freeway north of St. Ignace. We told him we could not accept the fawns and he should bring them back to where he found them because the mother was probably nearby and would be looking for them, unless she had been killed by a vehicle on the freeway. He explained that he had no idea where he found the fawns.

At the time, we had bottle-fed fawns walking around our gift shop with the tourists, so we could not bring in the fawns he picked up. We knew what had to be done. I got a large box to put the wild fawns in and placed the safely contained fawns in my truck, where they would be fine until closing time.

Next, we called wildlife rehabilitator Nora Kilpatrick, who lived in Lower Michigan about 15 miles south of us. She was not too happy to hear the reason for our call because she already had her quota of orphaned fawns. But her big heart could not say "no" to another one.

Nora would always call us when she had problems with fawns and didn't know what to do. We would supply advice, medicine and syringes, as she needed them.

The same year the guy in a suit left us with twin fawns, Nora called about a fawn a conservation officer had dropped off to her. She thought something was wrong with his legs because he always crouched as he walked. An even bigger problem is the young buck would not take a bottle; that is he wouldn't until she caught him in a landing net.

After we closed the DEER RANCH for the day, Sally and I headed for Nora's place with the box containing the twin fawns. When we arrived, we were greeted by Nora saying, "You are just in time. I have to feed the little guy."

She said she would go warm up the bottle of milk for the fawn and be out in a minute with the landing net. A few minutes later, when Nora came out of the door with bottle and net in hand, she was in for a surprise. I was sitting on a stump with the little guy lying in my lap sucking my finger.

"I don't believe this," she said. "From now on, you will be called the Deer Whisperer."

My experience dealing with fawns made it easy for me to catch that little buck fawn. I just went right in the pen he was in and picked him up. The trick was to move slowly and not do anything that might scare the fawn. There was nothing wrong with that fawn's legs. He simply crouched as Nora approached him because he was afraid of her. She may have made a quick movement when trying to catch him the first time, which scared him, making him leery each time she approached him.

A couple years later, Nora retired from the school system, so she could devote more time to the birds and animals she cared for. Nora did not get to enjoy retirement for very long. During the winter, Nora and her husband were preparing to go snowmobiling. With her machine running, Nora stepped in front of the machine and lifted the cover. The cover caught on the throttle cable and the machine surged forward into an automobile and crushed her. She died a short time later at the hospital, leaving behind her husband and many birds and animals.

As a tribute to our friend, we named our first doe fawn the next spring Nora.

October 26 & 27, 2010: The aftermath of 78 mph winds.

Chapter 15 ~ Hurricane Winds

You wouldn't think living in northern Michigan we would feel hurricane force winds, but we experience them quite often. St. Ignace is on the north side of the Straits of Mackinac, where Lakes Michigan and Huron come together and the distance between the Upper and Lower Peninsulas of Michigan is the shortest. Winds that build to high speeds across the open waters of the Great Lakes are sometimes funneled in our direction through the narrow gap between land masses.

November is one month when we often experience high winds. During that month in 2005, winds reached speeds of 75 miles per hour and caused problems at the DEER RANCH. We lost about 30 trees in that windstorm. One of those trees was a 60-foot spruce that came down on the fence of one of our deer pens. The fence came down with the tree, providing a means of escape for the deer that were in that pen.

The fence around pen number two was knocked down. All six deer that were in that pen got out and were roaming the walkways where the tourists normally walk around the pens. Due to the fact the ranch is double fenced, the deer were still inside the main fence, preventing them from escaping into the wild. That's why I'm glad the ranch is double fenced.

Once the problem was recognized, the large windblown spruce tree was removed and the fence was fixed, making the pen as good as new. Once that was done, we simply opened the gate to that pen and walked the deer back inside. Those strong winds tested our security system, which passed with flying colors. And the deer probably didn't mind a little change in scenery, being outside the pen looking in for a change.

Our strongest winds came during October 26 and 27 of 2010 when speeds of 87 miles per hour were recorded on the Mackinac Bridge. As a safety precaution, the bridge that connects the state's two peninsulas was shut down for many hours that day and into the night. Back at the DEER RANCH, where the wind speed was still 78 miles per hour, trees were coming down like rain as a result of that powerful wind, and some of them ended up on fences around the deer pens.

Sally and I were trying to cut those windblown trees off the fences, but so many trees were coming down around us that it got too dangerous to continue. As we ran back toward the gift shop and the shelter it provided, we went under the power lines just as three large cedar trees hit the wires, showering us with sparks. As we continued running toward safety, we heard a loud explosion as the transformer fuse blew.

We lost a total of about 60 trees in three of our pens during that windstorm. Fortunately, all of our deer came through the ordeal unscathed. We can't say the same about our double fence. We lost hundreds of feet of it that time.

The 8-foot-high double fence is made of wood and surrounds the deer pens, which are constructed from wire fencing that is 10 feet high. The outer fence prevents stray dogs, coyotes and wolves from seeing the deer. By the same token, the outer fence protects the deer from seeing canines that might pass by. The sight of a potential predator could cause the deer to panic. That's why it's important to have a fence that blocks their view.

Based on the weather forecast, we knew the windstorm was coming. To protect the big fiberglass deer in front of the ranch from possible damage, I chained it down the day before the strong winds hit. Although that precaution paid off, I should have also reinforced the nearby sign. The wind broke a 6x6 post that is part our sign.

During our 25 years at the DEER RANCH, we learned you have to have respect for the power of Mother Nature. When necessary, we just repair what she damages and go on to another day.

Pepper Spray

We mentioned in an earlier chapter about Bronco killing a couple does, and that I cut off his antlers to prevent that from happening again. The loss of his antlers was something that buck never forgot. Every time I came near the fence of the pen he was in he would snort at me and charge the fence. He never did this to anyone else. Whenever Bronco charged the fence when I was nearby, I gave him a shot of pepper spray on the nose. That helped calm him down.

Bronco charged the fence a second after I snapped this picture.

Chapter 16 ~ White Whitetails

The year was 1991 and the normally colored brown whitetails had been on exhibit at the Deer Ranch for 41 years. This was our third year of owning the Deer Ranch. Ed Gilkes with Ed's Archery, the guy who sold us Pepi in 1989, contacted us that year. This time, he wanted to sell us a yearling whitetail buck that was all white in color.

We liked the idea of having something different for the public to see. We thought such an unusual deer might attract more visitors to the DEER RANCH, too. So we agreed to buy our first white deer.

We named the leucistic deer Sno-Flake. Leucistic animals are white in color like albinos, but they have more pigmentation. Leucistic deer usually have normal colored brown eyes, for example, rather than pink eyes like albinos. Both leucistic and albino deer are color mutations of brown deer and either can have normally colored parents.

After we got Sno-Flake, we decided to put one of our does named Betty in with him to see how their fawns would turn out. Betty was mentioned in Chapter 2. As a fawn, she broke a hind leg that Sally and I helped her recover from. We figured Betty was a perfect mate for Sno-Flake because she was whitish-brown in color and had a lot of white on her legs.

Our hunch paid off. We were pleasantly surprised the following year when Betty gave birth to a white buck fawn that we named Sno-Ball. He was actually tan in color when he was born, so his white spots were visible just like those on a brown fawn would be. But when Sno-Ball was a year old and grew his summer coat, it was pure white like his father's.

The year that Sno-Ball grew his white coat, we purchased another white whitetail buck from Pennsylvania that was bottle-fed. His name was Blaze. Despite our best efforts to keep these white bucks apart, they ended up getting in a fight with their first sets of antlers, and one of them was hurt bad enough to require medical attention.

When we got Blaze, we kept him at our house while I constructed a new pen for him at the gift shop. It was a beautiful fall day when we thought it would be a good time to transfer Blaze from our house to his new pen. With Sno-Ball in pen four, we put Blaze in the newly created pen three. Pen three was created by splitting number four, so Blaze's new home had been part of Sno-Ball's stomping grounds.

As a yearling, Blaze didn't have much for antlers. Sno-Ball's antlers were larger even though he was the same age. One thing we noticed about our white whitetail bucks is they did not grow brow tines on their antlers. We had no genetic background on either buck, except the fact that they were not related.

After moving Blaze to the DEER RANCH, we decided to start pen number five on the back side of the other four pens. That would leave a six-foot walkway between the pens. With the rut starting, this was a good time to be working on an empty pen.

When we arrived at the DEER RANCH one morning that fall, we were surprised to find Sno-Ball in Blaze's pen fighting with him. The white yearling with the largest antlers had ripped a hole in the fence between his pen and the one occupied by Blaze to get at the smaller buck. Keep in mind that Blaze was occupying what had formerly been part of Sno-Ball's territory.

Blaze was a bloody mess due to the beating he was receiving from Sno-Ball and we were concerned about his welfare. Blood looks worse on a white deer than a brown one, of course. Fortunately, Blaze was not hurt as badly as we first thought he was. All of the blood on him was coming from a cut lip. In spite of the injury, Blaze was holding his ground against Sno-Ball.

I knew Blaze would still need medical attention, so I made a call to our veterinarian. Dr. Sara was 60 miles away, so I knew it would take an hour for her to get to the DEER RANCH. In the meantime, I thought about tranquilizing one of the white bucks, but if I did that, the one that wasn't darted would injure the one that was. I decided to try to separate the bucks.

Putting my pistol under my belt, just in case I needed it, I proceeded into the pen with the battling bucks. They were so busy with each other that they paid no attention to me as I approached. I'm sure they didn't even notice me. One of the first things I did is open the gate between pens three and four.

I then picked up a small log to distract the bucks. I tossed the log up in the air so it came down on their antlers. That surprised them enough that they backed away from one another. Once the bucks were separated, I chased Blaze into Sno-Ball's pen and shut the gate. I was then able to tranquilize Blaze without interference from Sno-Ball.

I was in the process of tying a wood pallet over the hole in the fence between pens three and four when Dr. Sara arrived. Ten stitches were required to close the cut on Blaze's lip. I washed blood from the buck's white coat with warm water to look for any other wounds and was pleased to find there were no others.

As long as Blaze was down, we decided to cut his antlers off. This made working conditions safer for me as I repaired the fence that Sno-Ball put a hole through. I put chain link fencing over the hole in the 4x2 wire fence to reinforce it. The repaired fence would be impossible for any buck to break through again.

By the time I got back to working on pen five it was December 26th and it was cold! The high temperature that day was nine below zero. The temperature was below zero every day. On February 11, the low temperature was 29 below zero. The high temperature that day reached 16 below zero, but we plowed on.

As a building contractor, we had to build motels during the winter, so the jobs were done before tourists arrived for the summer. We seemed to get more done in the winter because we had to work harder to stay warm.

With the white bucks that were part of our herd, we finally started getting a few white doe fawns born from different brown does. We kept records on how all of the deer were related to prevent any in-breeding. As the number of white fawns that were produced by our herd grew, we were able to start selling some of the white fawns. We were able to even donate a few white fawns to the Michigan Deer Breeders Association auction to help them out.

On one occasion, we were lucky enough to have one of our does give birth to triplets, all of which were white. That was the only time white triplets were produced. The genes favoring white fawns were common in matings between our leucistic bucks and brown does. In fact, white fawns occurred frequently with these pairings. The brown gene would only pop up every once in a while.

In cases where a white buck and doe mated, does would most often produce twins, with one being white and the other brown.

Chapter 17 ~ Our Albino Deer

After raising leucistic white whitetails for about 20 years, we never thought an albinistic whitetail would be a possibility in captivity. Some people that feed wild deer during the winter occasionally see an albino among the brown deer. The albinos that are seen are normally only visible for one winter then disappear.

ALF as a fawn

The reason for this is most albino deer do not live as long as normally colored whitetails because they often have other defects besides their coat color mutation. Some albinos don't have a good immune system, so any sickness could result in their death. Their white coloration also makes them more visible to predators. The lack of pigment in their eyes can affect their eyesight, too, making it more difficult for them to escape predators and avoid accidents.

The lack of pigment or melanin is responsible for albinism. That's why an albino deer's coat is white and its skin, hooves, nose and eyes are pink. The color or, more properly, the lack of color of a deer's iris is a true test of whether or not a whitetail is an albino. The iris of an albino deer appears pink due to the lack of pigment. The lack of color of the iris also makes it hard for the animals to see, as there is no color to refract the light coming in.

Because albinism is a recessive genetic trait, both parents must carry the recessive gene to produce an albino fawn. Both parents of an albino fawn may be normally colored even though they carry the gene for albinism. Most deer that carry genes for albinism are, in fact, brown in color because it is a recessive characteristic.

According to some estimates, one out of 30,000 fawns will be an albino. Boy, were we lucky. We beat those odds. Back in chapter 13 on TB testing, we introduced you to Brandi, our deer that we thought was a doe, but "she" had testicles under her skin.

After moving Brandi to pen five to be with a more aggressive buck named PEPI, we were surprised that what we thought was a doe still did not produce fawns. Dr. Sara discovered why Brandi didn't become pregnant even though the deer appeared to have all of the female parts necessary to have fawns. The news was a big disappointment for us. We decided to leave Brandi in pen five, giving up on the deer's potential to have fawns.

The following spring, as does were starting to get plump from their developing fawns, we noticed Brandi was also gaining weight. By then, we were convinced it would be impossible for the deer to be pregnant, so we thought something else was responsible for her weight gain. All of the does in pen five were brown, including Brandi, so we expected all of the fawns born in that pen to be brown as well, as they had been in the past.

Just when you think you have everything figured out about deer, they throw you a curve. As I was walking around the pens before opening the park one morning I was shocked to see a little white fawn nursing from its mother in pen five. The fawn's mother was lying on her side with her head down, which did not look right. I unlocked the gate to inspect the doe and was shocked to discover it was Brandi that had the white fawn. I was doubly shocked to determine Brandi had expired.

I ran back to the gift shop to tell Sally not to open the park until I removed Brandi and the fawn. Most deer farmers use old army stretchers to move deer, but since I was alone most of the time, I built a low two-wheeled cart to put deer on to move them. That made it possible for me to move deer by myself when I needed to. I was in for another surprise when I loaded the doe and fawn on the cart. I slid Brandi on first, and then placed the fawn on with her. As I did that, I noticed the fawn had pink eyes. This fawn was also pure white, unlike the tan colored white whitetails we were used to.

We had really beaten the odds. We had an albino fawn from a freak of nature that we never expected to give birth, and she gave birth to a freak of nature. Pepi and Brandi must have had the recessive genes for albinism. As Brandi got older, she must have produced enough female hormones to enable her to go into estrus and become pregnant. Having the fawn must have been such a drain on her system, however, that she didn't survive.

Kids in the park taking a white fawn for a walk

*When our gift shop clerk Katie **Steltzer** was about to graduate from high school, she requested that her school picture for the yearbook be with one of our white deer named Shadow.*

Twins - one white one brown

White whitetail triplets notice the white spots

A half hour later, I was holding our first albino buck fawn in the gift shop, amazed at how Mother Nature works sometimes. Since the albino was so rare, we wanted to increase its chances of survival, so we decided to bottle-feed it. We didn't want to risk putting the white fawn with another doe on the chance she might reject it. Worse yet, a potential foster mother could kill the fawn due to its white color.

When Alf was born, we were already bottle-feeding two fawns at our house, so we decided to keep Alf at the gift shop. Due to his poor eyesight, we thought he might run into furniture or something else at the house. He would be safer in the fawn pen. At the deer park, we had a fawn pen where we put bottle-fed fawns after they were weaned. The pen is 150 long and 12 feet wide, with a shelter at each end. That pen worked great for Alf.

It wasn't long before we learned that albino deer could get sunburned, so we had to keep Alf under a big tarp so he would always be in the shade. Shady days were okay to let him out. On sunny days, we put sunscreen on Alf's nose and ears. We did this for all seven years of Alf's life.

A few weeks after Alf was born, we decided he needed company. We were bottle-feeding a doe fawn named Hina. A little Japanese girl who saw Hina being born named her. We were told Hina means little flower.

Hina and Alf formed a close bond unlike any other bond between fawns that we ever raised. Alf would stick to Hina like glue. When she took off running, Alf would be right behind her. That behavior created a problem if and when she came to a sudden stop. Every time that happened, Alf would run into Hina.

When Alf was a yearling and sexually mature, we let him breed a few pigmented (leucistic) white whitetails, but those pairings didn't result in any albino offspring. We almost always got the more genetically dominant leucistic white whitetails. It wasn't until Alf turned five that he fathered an albino doe fawn that we named Sierra. We took her home with us to bottle-feed and give tender loving care.

We always had some all-important colostrum on hand that is essential for a fawn's first meals, and we certainly needed it in that case. I made sure the little fawn got as much colostrum as it needed soon after removing it from the pen where it was born. I wanted to do everything possible to make sure that fawn survived, and it worked. Before long the young albino buck was taking goat's milk from a bottle.

The first time our clerk Katie Steltzer saw the albino fawn she said he looked like an elf because the tips of his ears were bent down. We let her pick a name for this little guy. She named him Alf.

One of the first things we learned about Alf is that he had poor eyesight. That was obvious because he had a hard time finding a nipple. If he had been born in the wild and his mother survived, the white fawn's chances of survival might have been low due to this characteristic linked to his albinism.

ALF never grew brown tines

Siera waiting for bronco to be loaded for her trip downtown

Chapter 18 ~ Sierra, Our First Albino Doe

Sierra was born on May 29, 2009 to a pigmented white whitetail doe named Jamie. Our albino buck Alf was Sierra's dad. Jamie had twins, both of which were white in color. The second fawn was a leucistic white whitetail buck. Sally got to name the albino doe.

We had five gallons of milk replacer that we ordered from Indiana that we planned to feed Sierra. The milk replacer we got was advertised as the best on the market at the time. We left Sierra's brother with their mother.

Sierra was only on the commercial product a short time when she developed severe diarrhea. We had mixed the milk replacement as the directions instructed, but the liquid was so strong that it burned the hair off her legs and tail. We tried everything they recommended until Sierra started to refuse the bottle. Our veterinarian recommended giving the albino fawn a shot of Naxel every 12 hours and to start feeding her through a tube.

We got two gallons of goat's milk from a farm 40 miles north of us to start feeding Sierra through a tube. When feeding fawns through a tube, it's important to make sure the tube makes it all the way into their stomach. To confirm the feeding tube has reached the stomach, the free end is put in a cup of water to check for bubbles. When there's no bubbles, the feeding tube is where it's supposed to be.

Once the feeding tube was in place, I held Sierra's head up along with the end of the tube the milk was to go in. Sally would then insert a large syringe containing three ounces of milk into the tube and force the milk from the syringe down the tube. We fed Sierra this way five times a day for about a week until she got better. Then we switched back to feeding her from a bottle and she hooked right on. We were really glad that the tube feeding worked and that we didn't have to continue it any longer than we did. We prefer bottle-feeding our fawns.

We probably would have been better off feeding Sierra goat's milk to start with instead of the milk replacement product. The product certainly didn't work as well as it was supposed to. We were lucky we didn't lose that albino fawn.

To make sure Sierra didn't come into heat when she was six months old in November, we used a birth control product called Eustrumate. It was administered through a syringe in the form of a shot. We gave her three doses, one each month during November, December and January.

Healthy doe fawns could come into heat at six months of age. Since many doe fawns don't breed until December or January, they wouldn't give birth until September or October. A fawn born that late in the year would not have a winter coat by November when the weather turns cold. Consequently, they could freeze to death because the thin summer coat that they were born with does not have the insulation properties necessary to keep deer warm.

We used the same type of birth control we gave Sierra on a lot of fawns and had perfect success. The Eustrumate certainly worked on the albino doe. Although, as it turned out, she might have been sterile. Sierra never had a fawn during the time we owned the DEER RANCH. After we sold the place, the new owner said he found her dead in the corner of the barn one day. She may have gotten spooked for some reason and ran into the wall. The albino doe's eyesight was poor.

Most doe fawns that are bred when they are at six months old will produce a single fawn. If does don't get pregnant until they are 1 ½ years old, they will be two year old when having their first fawns and they will most often have twins.

There's a picture at the beginning of this chapter of Sierra during her first winter. The doe that was Sierra's mother (Jamie) had twin albino fawns the next year. The second photo shows those twin albinos. Sally used a tote bag from the North American Deer Farmers Association with two holes cut in the end to carry the fawns. Makes a great tote for hauling around twin fawns.

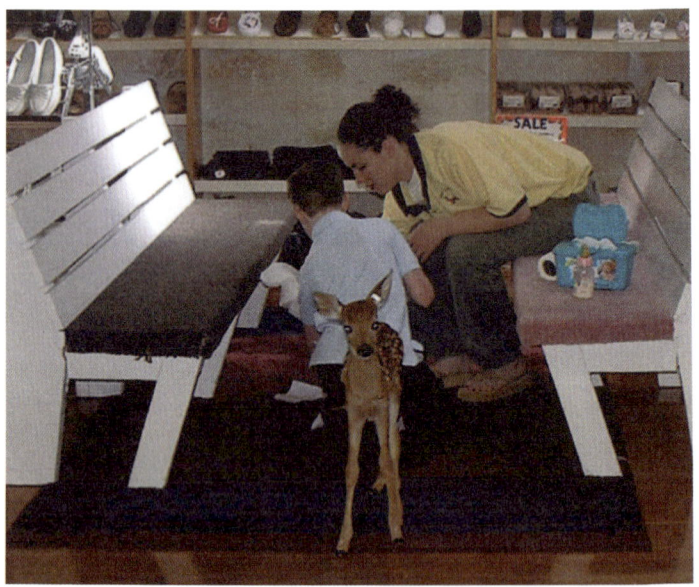

Clerk Heather Steltzer and Grandson Jacob Brown cleaning up after bottle feeding Kaila.

Grandson Jacob with Shadow

Chapter 19 ~ Bottle Feeding Fawns

As mentioned in chapter 5, we were forced to bottle-feed twin fawns Jacob and Autumn at our house during an extremely cold spring to keep them alive. The cold weather had claimed all of the other fawns born to our does that spring.

Although taking both fawns from their mother was good for them by increasing the newborns' chances of survival, doing so had a negative effect on the doe. Based on our observations, it is painful for the milk to dry up from her udder when no fawns are present to drink the milk her body has produced. Taking a doe's offspring from her also has an emotional toll. After carrying the developing fawns for 200 to 220 days, does are physiologically and instinctively geared to caring for their young. One year we watched a doe that lost a single fawn pace the fence for weeks, making moaning noises, as she appeared to grieve the loss of her stillborn fawn.

So when we decide to bottle-feed a fawn, we try to leave one with its mother, if she has twins. With one fawn to care for, the impact is not as great on does as when they are left with no young to take care of. Looking after even one fawn is enough to keep most does busy.

People frequently asked us why we want to bottle-feed fawns. It was necessary in some situations to increase their chances of survival like the circumstances Jacob and Autumn faced. The same was true for our first albino buck when his mother died after giving birth. Bottle-feeding fawns also makes them tame and easier to work with and handle at the DEER RANCH.

The tameness of bottle-fed fawns benefited our visitors, too. Many youngsters as well as adults, were able to touch and handle our bottle-fed fawns, adding to their experience. That would not have been possible if the fawns had not gotten used to being handled by people through us bottle-feeding them. It was always great to see kids interacting with our bottle-fed fawns after they had been placed in the fawn pen at the DEER RANCH.

During the years we operated the DEER RANCH, a total of 427 fawns were born to our does. Sally and I only named a handful of those fawns. We let our visitors name most of the fawns. Naming a fawn took on special significance when the people actually saw the animal being born.

To make sure newborns got the colostrum they needed from their mothers, we normally waited three days after a fawn was born before taking it for bottle-feeding. When fawns were removed from their mothers before three days had elapsed, a small donut ring usually appeared around their navels.

When we started bottle-feeding fawns, we put three ounces of milk in a bottle for each feeding. We fed fawns five times a day at four-hour intervals. The first feeding was at 6:00 am and they got their last bottle of milk for the day at 10:00 pm.

Besides providing milk as nourishment for bottle-fed fawns, we provided them with something else that will probably surprise most people. We always had a dish with dirt in it for the fawns to eat. The soil, which all fawns are exposed to in the wild, helped generate the stomach bacteria they needed to digest food.

After being fed, fawns also needed to be stimulated to get them to defecate and urinate. When a doe nurses her fawns, she licks under their tail at the same time to stimulate elimination. We use wet wipes to toilet train our bottle-fed fawns. After they are done drinking, we tickle them with a wet wipe and they poop in the wipe. The soiled wipe is then flushed down the toilet.

We lay down paper towels next and tickle them with another wet wipe to get them to urinate. By using this procedure, we have had very few accidents in the house after bottle-feeding 17 fawns. The fawns get used to being stimulated before defecating or urinating and don't eliminate waste from their bodies between feedings.

After 50 days of bottle-feeding, most fawns are weaned. That's when we brought them to the fawn pen at the DEER RANCH. We usually waited until the rut was over to introduce bottle-fed fawns to the other deer.

On a typical day when we had fawns we were bottle-feeding, I got out of bed before 6:00 am. The first thing I did was to get the coffee going and then warm milk for the fawns. I wouldn't have time to get the coffee on before those little fawns were by my feet looking for breakfast.

The ceramic heated floor of our kitchen posed a problem for the fawns because it was slippery for their little hooves to navigate. Most of the fawns managed to learn to get around on the slippery surface, however, after a few slips and slides. One fawn named Shadow couldn't seem to master that slippery floor until I came up with something to help him with the problem. That was to put sticky pads on his hoofs. I used the foam pads that fit on nosepieces of eyeglasses for Shadow's hooves. I put two pads on each hoof. They worked wonders for Shadow's mobility in our kitchen.

Each fawn we bottle-fed was fitted with a collar or a harness that we could attach a leash to. We could then take the fawns for a walk on a leash just like a dog. After the morning feeding and toilet duties they would go outside for a walk or run. They were then loaded into the truck for a day in the gift shop.

At the store, the fawns had the run of the place. They didn't actually do much running. Because all of the floors in the store were varnished wood, the fawns had to learn to walk slow to avoid slipping and sliding. The fawns had to be watched closely when customers came in the door because they loved to sneak out the door to the large front porch, where they would lay on the couch, watch the traffic go by and greet tourists as they came in.

Sally and I didn't normally sit down for supper each day until 8:00 or 8:30 pm. After closing the DEER RANCH to the public, we made sure all of the deer in the park were taken care of. We then loaded the bottle-fed fawns in the truck and headed for town for supper. Once we hit the road, the fawns would lie down and behave better then most kids.

Sometimes after supper, we would stop at the local ice cream shop for a cone. If the girls who were working there saw the truck, they would greet us with a dish of soft serve vanilla ice cream for the fawns.

Although most of the fawns we bottle-fed at our house stayed for 50 days, at least one fawn's stay was cut short when its behavior got out of line. Sally routinely went home to take care of various tasks during the course of the day. One day she returned to the store quicker than expected. When she got back, she announced that Shadow was no longer welcome as a guest at the house.

When Sally went home that day, Shadow was not behind my easy chair where he normally was. That was his favorite hiding place. She found him standing on the bed, which was covered with her best bedspread. That behavior resulted in his transfer to the fawn pen earlier than normal.

I knew I was in charge of the deer, but when it came to the house, Sally called the shots. The following year, we had two more fawns in the house for fifty days, but their behavior was better than Shadow's had been. The 17 fawns we bottle-fed in the house over the years became as tame as a dog. That proved beneficial to us and the tourists who stopped to see our deer.

A tourist family with Kaila

A buck named 30/30 hiding in the weeds

Whitetail Deer Facts

Type: Mammal

Diet: Herbivore

Average life span in captivity: 6 to 14 years

Size: 6 to 7.75 ft (1.8 to 2.4 m)

Weight: 110 to 300 lbs (50 to 136 kg)

Group name: Herd

Did you know? "White-tailed" refers to the white underside of the deer's tail, which it displays and wags when it senses danger.

Chapter 20 ~ Odds & Ends

When we bought the DEER RANCH in 1988, I started taking notes with the idea of writing a book about our experiences. There were a lot of little things of interest that I wasn't able to fit into previous chapters. Here is a small sampling:

Dental

Whitetails don't often have problems with their teeth, but one day I found a doe with a swollen jaw and decided we should get the veterinarian involved. After the doe was tranquilized by Dr. Sara, she informed me that the doe had a bad tooth that had to be pulled. The Dr. removed the tooth then gave the doe a shot of antibiotics and the reversal drug. The deer was back on her feet and never knew what happened. Of the hundreds of deer we have had, this was the first and only dental problem we ever had.

Lice

This was something new for us when we discovered a raccoon in the feed box for the deer in one of our pens. I live trapped the raccoon to remove him. After the raccoon was in the trap, it looked like it had mange, but it must have been infested with lice. Before long the deer in that pen had lice. Those deer were all bottle-fed, so it was easy to rub lice powder all over them to get rid of the parasites. I also gave those deer a shot of medicine to help get rid of the lice.

The Parade

During the years we owned the DEER RANCH, we often participated in an annual parade held during late June in association with the St. Ignace Car Show. It's called the "Down Memory Lane" Parade, which takes place on Friday evening along the city's main street during the car show weekend. The giant fiberglass deer that at all other times was securely positioned in front of the DEER RANCH, was our main attraction in the parade.

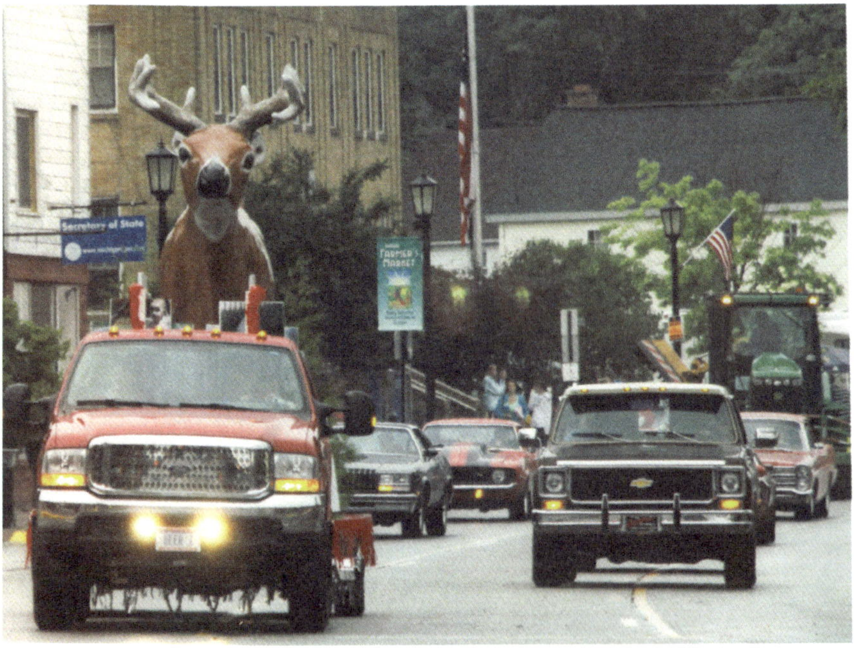
Secretary of State

WORLDS OLDEST LIVE WHITETAIL EXHIBIT
1950 60 YEARS 2010

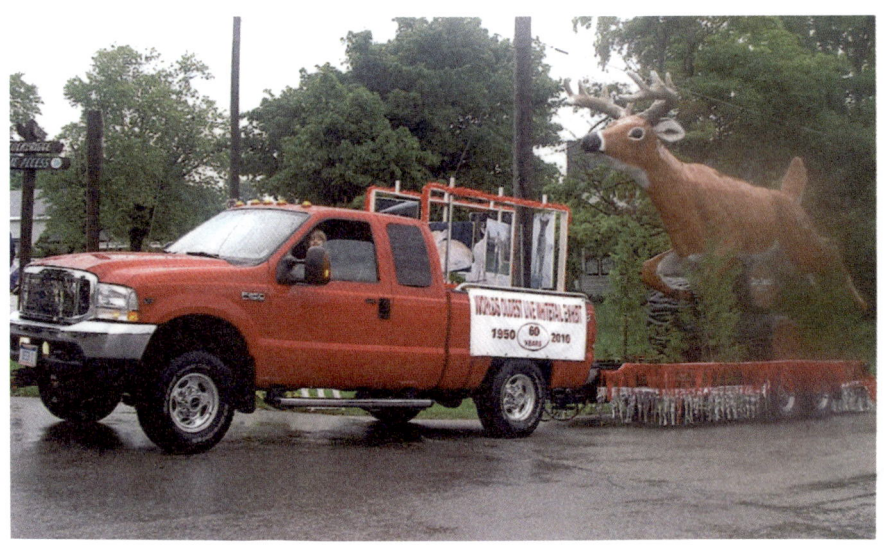

One year we had two of our store clerks sitting under the large deer, each holding a bottle-fed fawn. We did not take any pictures that year since you don't get to see the parade when you are in it.

After the parade was over, we always returned the large running fiberglass deer to its concrete base in front of the DEER RANCH, so we would be ready for business the next morning. Loading and unloading the fiberglass deer was actually easy. We used plastic pipes for rollers to move the statue to and from the base. The deer weighed about 800 pounds, but it only took two of us to load and unload it.

The annual car show is one of the biggest events in St. Ignace every summer. The show was started in 1976 when 138 cars participated. Now there are over 1,000 entries of antique, custom and celebrity automobiles, all of which are on display in town during the weekend.

Bad feed

When we got a load of deer pellets delivered to our silo, I got in the habit of climbing a ladder to the top of the silo to grab a handful of the pellets as they were unloaded. One time I did this, the pellets were lighter in color than normal. I then tasted a couple of the pellets, as I normally did, and they tasted bitter.

After all of the pellets were unloaded, the driver told me the guy at the Purina Plant had put too much of an ingredient in the food, but it should still be okay. Deer are usually good at determining what is good for them to eat. A day later we noticed the deer would not eat any of these pellets. After a few phone calls we found out they put too much calcium in this batch of pellets.

So we had to empty three tons of pellets from the silo with five gallon buckets. The feed store brought us bags of pellets to feed our deer until they could mix another large load of pellets. The Purina Feed Mill we bought the pellets from was 175 miles to the south. They replaced the bad batch of pellets.

First Prize

One of our customers sent us a picture that they had taken while visiting the Deer Ranch and we got permission to use it. We entered the picture in a photo contest put on by the North American Deer Farmer and won first place in the buck category.

First Prize! "Dad just wait till I grow antlers."
Photo by Jennifer VanderKlok

Warts

Deer can get everything a human can get and warts is one of them. One of our bottle-fed bucks named Bronco had a wart and everyone who saw it said it would eventually fall off. Not willing to wait for the wart to fall off, I found an easier way to get rid of it that didn't involve surgery.

The wart was high on his back hip. Because this buck was tame, I came up with a way to stop the blood flow to the wart. I used dental floss to tie tightly around the base of the wart. Once the blood flow was stopped to the wart, it was gone in no time.

Deer Ranch Sold

During 2011, someone made us an offer to buy the Deer Ranch that we couldn't refuse. So we sold the tourist attraction, enabling us to retire at the age of 70. Retirement didn't last long though.

In 2012 I got a new license to raise deer and bought two fawns to bottle-feed. We started **Martin Lake Deer Farm** to give us something to do during our retirement. We will be starting our 26th year raising whitetails during 2013.

Martin Lake Deer Farm
(Breeding for Predictability)
W 1522 E Martin Lake Road
St. Ignace, MI 49781
906-643-9311
Owners Harold and Sally Kriesche

About the Author
Harold Kriesche

Born and raised in Upper Michigan, I started my teen years hunting and trapping with my father, who spent most of his life in the woods and was the best teacher around. When I was 14, my father would drop me off at a lake where I would spend a week in a tent while trapping muskrats. Back then there were no cell phones to call home, so you waited until it was time to get picked up or walk 10 miles to get home. I was a building contractor for 45 years besides owning the Deer Ranch with my wife Sally. Since we got into raising whitetails in 1988 I have kept a journal on our deer and this is what prompted me to write this book. A lot of our customers said that I should write a book because of my knowledge about deer. I don't proclaim to be an expert on deer since we all learn as we go, and each deer breeder has his own way of doing things. Now that we are not exhibiting deer to the public, we will be raising deer for the best genetics.

Where's the bottle dad!

In closing we just want to say that deer farming is a very rewarding business and is the fastest growing business out there today. It can be a little like the building trade where you eat chicken one week but sometimes feathers the next week. You can make a living deer farming if you buy good genetics, it cost the same to feed a cheap deer or a good proven genetic deer.

God gave us these wonderful animals and you have to respect them and their different traits. We learned early not to ever go into our pens from October until after the antlers fall off. I always carry a 40 cal. Pistol or we tranquilize the buck before entering a pen. Even with a bucks antlers cut off he can still do damage. A bottle fed buck is the most dangerous because he has no fear of humans. Most deer farmers do not bottle feed bucks for this reason.